· D A N ·

· Written by Jenny Hessell · Illustrated by Diane Beyk ·

wrung roNg

For Matthew who also ran away

One day Daniel's teacher said,
"Daniel Hitchens,
you are an *atrocious* speller!"

3

Daniel ran home.
He shut himself in his room
with a note pinned on his door.
It said:

KEEP OUT!
~~atrochus~~
utroshis
terrible speller
inside

Daniel's mother knocked on the door.
"Can I come in?" she asked.

"No," said Daniel.
"Go away."

So she did.

No! Go away!

Daniel's father knocked on the door.
"Can I come in?" he asked.

"No," said Daniel.
"Go away."

So he did.

Daniel's brother and sister
climbed up to the window
and pressed their noses
against the glass.
"Can we come in?" they asked.

"No!" shouted Daniel.

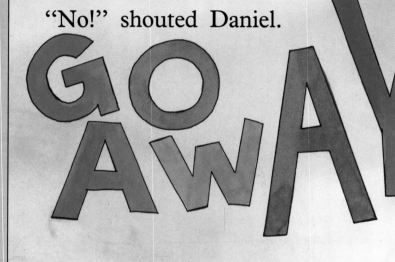

So they did.

The next morning,
Daniel's mother phoned the school.
"I'm afraid Daniel won't be there today,"
she said.
She told them what had happened.

That afternoon, a note arrived
from Daniel's teacher.
It said:

Dear Daniel,
Since you ran away,
everything has gone
~~rong~~ ~~wrung~~ wrong.
It's been horrible !
Please come back.
Love from Miss Jones.

So he did.